An Ode to
Yesterday

Daphne Xulu

BookLeaf Publishing

India | USA | UK

Presentation by *BookLeaf Publishing*

Web: www.bookleafpub.com

E-mail: info@bookleafpub.com

ISBN: 9789357691970

First edition 2022

DEDICATION

I dedicate my creativity to Katherine.

Without your love, strength and commitment I would not be here, loving you fuels my determination to succeed. Thank you for the gift of life, the gift of loving and the gift of resilience. I am forever grateful to be your daughter.

My successes are your successes.

ACKNOWLEDGEMENT

I wish to acknowledge the people I have had relationships and grievances with, for without you, this book would not exist. You may know who you are, or you may not. Perhaps, either way, it doesn't matter.

PREFACE

"All you have to do is write one true sentence. Write the truest sentence that you know."

Ernest Hemingway

Time Unseen

I write where the flowers bloom,
in the alcove under the moon.
I write to the downpour of rain,
and I lose myself again.
Lost to the land of sailors' dreams,
where ships sink and sirens scream.

Screams to streams, water to red;
ocean to river, the water flows.
Dawn and dusk and the darkness grows,
I wallow in the morning yellow.
From below the ground groans:

"I am home. I am home. I am home.

Home is alone where the weeds grow,
and cattle roam in the farmer's green.
Home is somewhere between the mud road
tracks
and evergreen -

home is lost in time unseen."

I close my eyes and I see the faces,
faces of friends, faces of strangers passed,
faces of the dead, faces of ancient dread.

I remember the day I lost my head -

the day the reaper declared home dead.

Home

Dawn broke over the cliffs,
a hazy yellow; red and gold.
Sunlight was here and I was old.

I paused, I waited, I wanted,
I danced under the waning moons;
and I cried in April, May and June,
I cried for the warmth of you.

Tired feet ache,
and tired hearts fade,
and under the bright lights of day,
I see you.
I see beyond the pain.

I see home, glistening in the morning dew.
I know your name and I carry these chains,
I'll be there soon.

I walk the stretch, the lonesome mile,
I trudge these steps;
and last night I looked into the dark.
The stars were blue;
they painted my way to you.

And I found myself,
somewhere in that midnight dream,
and I knew-

Home is you.

Concrete

Something is stirring in the sky,
the sun looks like nirvana,
and I'm living in a world without an end.

Bloodlines run through the heavens tonight,
and there's nothing left to burn.
The city is empty,
 and I walked on out,
out across the urban scape.
I touch the rooftops,
I bid my escape.

I came here back in the old times,
a reincarnation of love.,
I came for a fight.

I'm taken by the wind.
I fly across the boroughs,
 I'm letting go,
and there's nothing left.

I'm taken by the wind.
I can't touch the ground,
 I can't reach the clouds,
I am lost, arms crossed, feet to frost;

I am lost within.

I came here to find love,
I found it caught in the trees,
his heart in the city park,
and now there's nothing left.

Fate took me away,
up and away and I plummet down.
Cheek on concrete,
concrete on cheek,
I am crumpled, I am dead.

This home is lost to me,
the pavements turn red.

Ten to Two

Darkness struck at ten to two,
and I'm sorry I'm no longer here.
Lost in the confusion,
I whisper to the night,
and somewhere back along,
I disappeared.

I look at the clock,
the clock on the wall,
and the arms they tick,
and I'm gone again,
on a timeless adventure,
to God knows where.

I inhale the smoke,
I drag my last cigarette,
and I welcome the end.
I'm cloaked in darkness,
and the black smothers me,
goodbye, my friend.

I knew you well.

I lived here once,
now never again.

I walked the streets,
I smelled the scene.
The air is incense and I'm in a dream;
a dream of friends who have never been,
dreams of disease
and the hellbent breeze.

Into the Bleak

The bus trundles through the countryside,
 its monotonous melody promising parting.
Its engine purrs to the pledge of an unknown
start.

And, the wind whips through the trees;
the branches, I can hear them, whispering out to
me.
They scratch the windows; they etch our names.
Raindrops run to blood, and blood to disdain.

The bus turns to flames, red tongues licking hot.
Skin on fire, eyes to soot; melting sockets.
Dreaming, a scorching desire.

We burn hot in here.

My steely eyes smoulder through your demise,
your face in the flames; mine unharmed.

I spit your name to extinguish the flames,
the saliva of the survivor to drown the blaze.

Rain plummets down now, hitting heavy.
I watch it lash the windows.

I don't feel anything,
I am nothing.
It's dark now and the ghost of yesterday follows
the road.

The rain drowns out the inevitable,
head-lights blurry, red and blue,
no man wins, we all lose.

The bus disperses to a thousand stars,
stars of purple and stars of pink,
stars of the forgotten and stars of me.

Merciless mishaps turn into a sedative,
and I am asleep, I am at peace.

If I were a romantic, I'd see you there,
amongst the stars.
But we lost sight of it all,
and now the planets hang us from their heavenly
strings.
We swing, our feet tied and our necks limp,
we hang lifelessly.

I see the faces of you and me,
I feel the breaking of the hearts,
the hearts that starved us
.... till death do us part.

And we fall.
We fall with the autumn,
 we fall with the noon,
we fall and we unite.

We wither because we are obsolete.
We fall from the winter, into the bleak.

The fall

I remember.

I remember the wall
where the flowers crawl;
the ice-cold winds,
and they fall.

I remember the scent,
the scent of death,
the pungent rotting petals.

Petals to leaves,
leaves to earth –
Earth to us all.

The fall of the flowers,
the fall of the reds and blues,
the fall of nature, the fall of all.

I remember the flowers –
they crawled up the walls.

They crawled, I crawled –
they died, I died,
death to us all.

The Woods

Away to the woods:
he beckoned her.

Away to the woods:
she pleaded.
He beckoned:
she called.

Away to the woods,
his howl hoarse.
She strayed.

Where is away?
How far?
How distant?
How frequent,
a promise broken?

Where are you?
You are away.
Away, away, away.

I loved you once:
she cried.
I love you still:

he died.

Decades passed:
time gone.
Into the woods,
she called him.

He called her name.

Relate

I laugh because I relate.
I laugh as I stumble over city rats
and the gutter ghouls.

I laugh down dark alleys
 and at the garden graves,
I laugh because I relate.

I skip over midnight cobbles
and the runaway strays.
I tear through the streets,
past men and violence.

I laugh as I dart,
past missing person posters,
and bank robbers on the run.

I become the wind,
whipping wedding bells,
and whistling with death.

Death swings one stroke at a time,
a pendulum of life.
We're puppets on a string,
a string of strife.

And I laugh because I relate.

Hatred

The footpath is muddled,
muddied reds and browns.
Blood from Satan,
his veins run through the ground.

Your head emerges from the branches,
your eyes shovelled ten feet down.

I don't love you and everyone is crying,
you're far from me, your body dying.

I dye you with soot, I paint you with dread.
His hands reach out, he strangles you,
you splutter, you are dead.

"I hate him", I said to the stars,
"I hate him, God".
I hate you too, you and the tears you shed.

Leaves crumble and fall,
and darkness smothers all around.
Covered in your lies,
my skin peels off and I die.

I die , I die , I die.
I die as long as you're alive.

The Candle

The candle burns bright,
in the quiet spaces in the dark.
Its yellow light
turns to orange and flickers to red.

When the hour strikes and the seconds tick,
when I wear my chains over bulging veins,
which pulse in woe,
when I'm shackled to the shadow,

I hear you.
I feel you.
I haven't forgot.

When the rain rattles the windows,
and the wind howls like ghouls,
the candle's flames lick and lash,
and grow.

When the last bell rings out,
and the clothes submerged in the liquid
of love and loss, and life is wrung,
the candle sizzles on.

In dreary afternoons,

and when the suns turn to moons,
when the wails and cries,
and far out screams die,
when the chaos subsides,

I see you.
I feel you.
I haven't forgot.

Flowers

The flowers died,
the ones by the church,
wilted grey.
The flowers died,
the ones you picked for me,
I lost them along the way.

Love is Thunder

I see him at the window
rasping at the glass.
I see him in the night,
howling at the pane,
howling at last.

Grief

The day dawns and I am sad.
The day dawns and I am glad.

The day dawns, and snow twinkles white,
the air is sharp and I already crave the night.

For why live in the day,
when you can dwell in the dark?
Why discover yourself scatter-brained,
 and half alive,
 buried in contempt, and homing a disguise?

Why succumb to the sun,
when the stars are bright?

I dance in the warmth.
I cry in the cold.

The night comes and I am sad.
The night comes and I am glad.

The Moving Van

This is where I told you I was leaving you.
This door, the barrier between everything,
and nothing.

The divide between you and me,
a wooden frame which shut out hope,
and rendered it true
that you,
you would never change.

This is where I told you I was leaving you,
in the quiet afternoon,
the neighbours went away,
and the old man croaked.
The roads quietened, and the moving van
rumbled.

The whole world knew it had crumbled.
And, this is where I told you I was leaving you,
and you knew I knew,
that you,
you would never change.

Sunken Darkness

I stand here, I stand in the dark.
My eyes, do not see,
my past, it's lost to me.

I stand here, your grave, dug here.
In the sunken darkness I hear:
your fears.

I hear your broken heart.
It beats beneath me,
it beats here.

What is it to love?
That's what you asked me;
you begged to know.

I can't say, for if I had loved,
you wouldn't be here,
beneath this dirt.

Alive in the Morning

Alive in the morning:
echoes and etches,
and parting dawning.

Alive in the morning:
eyes tired,
soul weak,
slumberous breaths of
gone by weeks.

Alive in the morning:
no sleep,
no worries,
no woes.

Alive in the morning:
in our clouded world of
love and poetry,
of loss
and yearning.

Alive in the morning:
after a night of
forgotten fawning.

Insomnia

I close my eyes,
the day cracking through the blinds.

A moving world awakes outside,
car wheels splattering puddles.

Soft is the sound of harsh rain,
the chugging of the city train.

A city which awakes at dawn,
and beeps and honks and crawls.

A city who sleeps through the night,
a moving world of the rest and I.

Taken

Floating on water,
taken by the sea.
Sun-soaked body,
I slip free.

Drifting over waves,
peace of mind,
reminiscent beauty,
I am blind.

Far from land,
alone with the tide,
prisoner of time,
I abide.

Blood Moon

I see the moon,
between the trees,
it breathes.

The blood moon bleeds.
Its gurgling breaths,
a silent caress.
It bleeds for you and me.

America

Midnight magic rained down,
stardust ashes of red white and blue.

Catherine wheels exploded,
spiralling electrified cries.

Whistles and whirs,
 and catalytic bangs
 of blue lakes and orange suns.

Grey roads and yellow lines,
flying grit of Miami heat dazzled,
and pink hearts exploded
 across the black sky.

The moon became home to bud lights,
and burgers,
of snow boots,
canteen food
and far away friends.

And as my clammy face
blotted pink,
I marvelled at my life.

A bolt of lightning seared
through the stars,
and struck me down.

I was celebrating youth
and tight-skinned freedom.
I was partying to the ways of the world,
of the roaming journey of the

mad
mad
mad.

I applauded wide-eyed monsters of love,
and cold creatures of chaos.

I gathered the weeds and turned them red,
sewing fields of poppies and primroses:

of petals and pearls,
of boisterous yearning
and forgotten grieving.

Bath

I sat in the square at Bath Abbey,
the sun warming the Georgian stone,
the windows of the abbey glinting.

An opera singer,
on her knees,
hands extended to the sky,
belting Time to Say Goodbye.

Maybe she was right.
It was time to say goodbye.
For its always good,
to listen to a sign.

And I was almost moved to tears,
as a small girl with pigtails
and red shoes ran across the shadow,
towards the light.

But I decided,
too many tears had been shed,
and I was moved in silence,
my silence, instead.

www.ingramcontent.com/pod-product-compliance
Lightning Source LLC
LaVergne TN
LVHW010933200726
843509LV00013B/2197